Meet Kamala Harris

By Nia Hence

Illustrated by Winda Mulyasari

For Blomie, Mable, Margie, Ashley, Latricya and all the other strong women in my family.

Meet Vice President Kamala Harris. She is the first woman, first African-American and first Asian-American to be Vice President.

Kamala Devi Harris was born October 20, 1964, in Oakland, California.

1964, oakland. california

She was the first child to her Jamaican-born father and her Indian-born mother.

Her father, Donald Harris, was a professor and her mother, Shyamala, a cancer researcher.

Kamala was brought up in a multicultural home. Her mother made sure both of her cultures were embraced. She also attended both a Black Baptist Church and a Hindu Temple.

She often shared her culture with others. She would bring her black friends home, share Indian food and paint Henna on their hands.

Kamala spent summers in India
visiting family and learning about her
culture.

Her grandfather, PV Gopalan, was a high-ranking government official and fighter for independence. He was one of the people who had a heavy influence on her.

YELLOW HOUSE

Kamala's parents divorced when she was seven years old. Afterward, she lived with her mother and sister, Maya, in a yellow house. The three of them became very close because of this.

In school, Kamala was a good student. To get to school each day, she traveled on a long bus ride across town. She did this to go to a better school and have more opportunities.

Her family later moved to Montreal, Canada when she was 12, for her mother's new job.

MONTREAL

When she was 13 years old, she followed her parents to the path of activism. She and her sister, Maya, led a demonstration at their apartment building to protest kids being unable to play on the lawn. They were successful in their feat.

The school Kamala attended was a French-speaking school. She finished high school there in Canada, but went back to the U.S. for college.

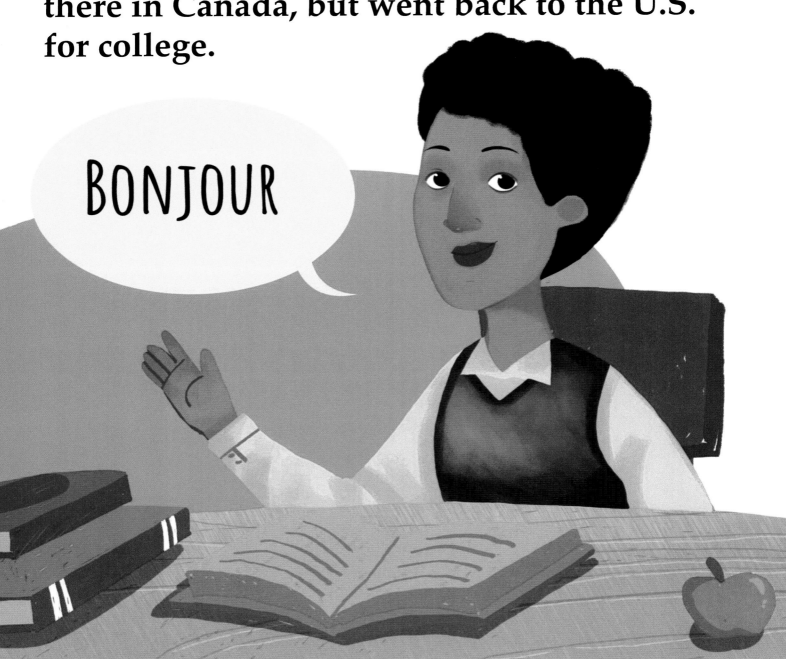

She chose to attend Howard University, a top HBCU. She majored in political science and economics and joined the sorority Alpha Kappa Alpha.

After college, Kamala went on to finish law school at California Hastings College of Law. She then became a lawyer and later California's first black woman District Attorney.

As the District Attorney, she created the "Back on Track" program to help people who made terrible mistakes, get job training and make a better life for themselves

In 2016, Kamala became a US Senator for California. She was the first South Asian-American to do this. And the second African-American woman.

She married her love, Doug Emhoff in 2004 and is called Momala by his two children, a pet name they have for her.

Other things you should know about Kamala Harris.

She loves to cook.

She loves hip hop music.

She collects Chuck Taylor shoes.

She loves to read.

She has written three books. One of them is a children's book.

And last, her mother is her greatest inspiration. She takes her motto from her.

"You may be the first to do many things but make sure you're not the last."

- Shyamala Gopalan Harris

Made in the USA
Las Vegas, NV
29 September 2024

95983625R00021